RYA CEV

Illustrations by Andrew Simpson

© Robert Gibson
First Published 2010
The Royal Yachting Association
RYA House, Ensign Way, Hamble
Southampton SO31 4YA
Tel: 0844 556 9555
Fax: 0844 556 9516
E-mail: publications@rya.org.uk
Web: www.rya.org.uk
ISBN: 978-1-906435721
RYA Order Code: G106

A CIP record of this book is available from the British Library.

Note: While all reasonable care has been taken in the preparation of this
book, the publisher takes no responsibility for the use of the methods or
products or contracts described in the book.

Technical Editor: Andrew Norton
Cover Design: Tony Collins
Photographs: DBA, The Barge Association, Christian and Charlotte Huber
Typesetting and Design: Kevin Slater
Proofreading and indexing: Alan Thatcher
Printed in China through World Print

Totally Chlorine   Sustainable
Free   Forests

THE ICC CEVNI TEST

A valid ICC (International Certificate of Competence) is often required for cruising Europe's inland waters. To validate your ICC for inland waters you must take the CEVNI test, which checks your knowledge of the rules and signs that skippers of pleasure craft are expected to know and follow.

Taking your CEVNI test

The information in this book will give you a great start to preparing for your CEVNI test. You could also have a go at the practice test that's available on our RYA Interactive website (www.ryainteractive.org.). You can practise there as much as you like before committing to the real test.

When you feel ready to take the test, contact a test centre and they can arrange it for you. You can find a list of them on www.rya.org.uk. Click on 'Where's My Nearest' at the top of the home page and then search for ICC test centres.

There are two ways to take the test – online or on paper.

Taking the test online means you can take it anywhere, anytime, so long as you have an internet connection. When you search for ICC test centres on our website you simply need to tick the option for ICC CEVNI Test (Online). Any one of the centres listed can give you access to the test.

If you would prefer to take the test on paper, you will need to travel to an ICC test centre. To find your nearest centre, go to the 'Where's My Nearest' page, select 'ICC Test Centre' in the 'Show me' box and tick the option for ICC CEVNI Test (Paper) and then enter your postcode.

Wind   Tidal stream or current

Key to symbols used in illustrations throughout the book

INTRODUCTION

Navigation on the interconnected European inland waterways system is regulated by the 'Code Européen des Voies de la Navigation Intérieure' (CEVNI rules). It is essential that boaters setting forth on those waters have a working knowledge of the rules. Happily there are many similarities between the CEVNI rules and the IRPCS (International Regulations for the Prevention of Collision at Sea) with which most boaters will be familiar. The signs (of which there are many) found on the inland system follow a regular pattern, so newcomers to the delights of the inland waterway system should not be daunted.

It should be borne in mind that some European inland waterways carry significant amounts of large commercial traffic, so an understanding of the rules followed by that traffic is necessary for your own safety.

The CEVNI code was introduced in 1985 under the auspices of the United Nations in order that Boat masters of various nationalities could communicate with each other and understand their actions without the need to speak a common language.

Rob Gibson

CONTENTS

WHERE THE RULES APPLY

The CEVNI rules apply on the 'interconnected' system of canals, rivers, lakes and other broad waters in Continental Europe.

On canals the rules apply above (uphill of) the first lock, while on rivers they apply above (upstream of) the Tidal Limit.

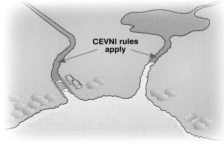

CEVNI rules apply

ORIENTATION

If you enter the inland waterway system from the sea, you will find that the system of lateral buoys continues upstream, with red can buoys on your port side and green conical buoys on your starboard side.

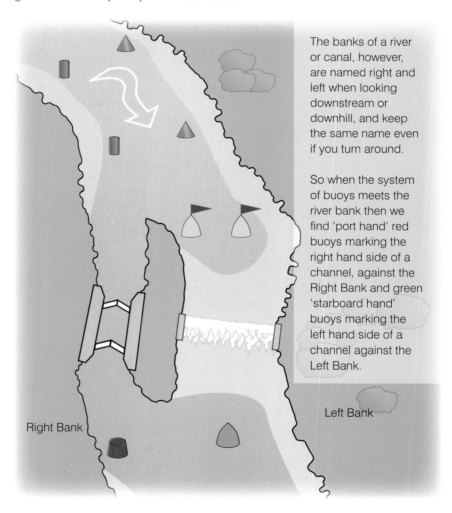

The banks of a river or canal, however, are named right and left when looking downstream or downhill, and keep the same name even if you turn around.

So when the system of buoys meets the river bank then we find 'port hand' red buoys marking the right hand side of a channel, against the Right Bank and green 'starboard hand' buoys marking the left hand side of a channel against the Left Bank.

Right Bank

Left Bank

PRINCIPLES OF SIGNS

There are many signs on the banks of European rivers and canals. They are used to control the passage of commercial and leisure vessels alike. The signs fall into six categories, each with a different style and colour scheme. So if you don't recognise a particular sign you should be able to work out, from the style, whether it says 'do' or 'don't'. Here are the six categories with an example of each:

MANDATORY
Square or rectangular, red and white, usually with a red border.
Signs that must be obeyed.

AUTHORISATIONS
Green and White boards and green flags or lights.
Saying 'go', or 'pass this way'.

PROHIBITIONS
Red and White, often with a red diagonal stripe. Designating actions that you must not take.

RECOMMENDATIONS
A variety of styles, signalling the best way to proceed.

RESTRICTIONS
Square with red borders.
Detailing physical restrictions or limitations.

INDICATIONS
Blue square or rectangular signs, providing information and indicating permitted activities.

In general terms then:

■ Red, or Red and White signs and lights, must be obeyed and will tell you where you cannot go, or cannot do.

■ Green lights, or Green and White signs tell you when and where you can go.

■ Blue signs tell you where you can do things.

LIGHTS

(Traffic Lights are used as signals, to control the movement of vessels, and provide information.)

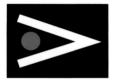

No entry to the side arm or port

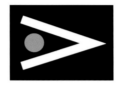

Entry permitted to the side arm or port

Passage Authorised

Warning – vessels emerging from a side arm

Do Not Make a Wash

No Passage but prepare to get underway

Prolonged Stoppage

Short Term Stoppage

Stop as required by the regulations

You may proceed

Passage permitted for vessels of a reduced height, two way traffic

MANDATORY SIGNS

Red bordered signs that MUST be obeyed.

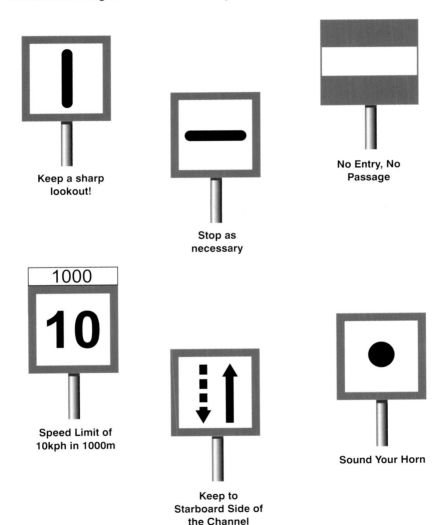

Keep a sharp
lookout!

Stop as
necessary

No Entry, No
Passage

Speed Limit of
10kph in 1000m

Keep to
Starboard Side of
the Channel

Sound Your Horn

PROHIBITIONS and RESTRICTIONS

Red or Red and White signs often with a red diagonal stripe. These signs describe actions that you MUST NOT take or advise of physical restrictions, or limitations to navigation.

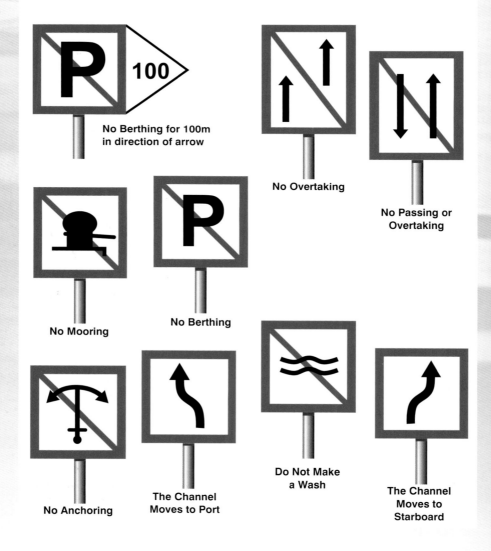

No Berthing for 100m in direction of arrow

No Overtaking

No Passing or Overtaking

No Mooring

No Berthing

No Anchoring

The Channel Moves to Port

Do Not Make a Wash

The Channel Moves to Starboard

AUTHORISATIONS

Green, or Green and White signs, flags and lights, authorising passage.

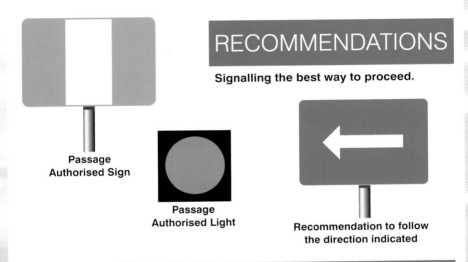

Passage
Authorised Sign

RECOMMENDATIONS

Signalling the best way to proceed.

Passage
Authorised Light

Recommendation to follow
the direction indicated

INDICATIONS

Blue signs providing information and indicating where activities CAN take place.

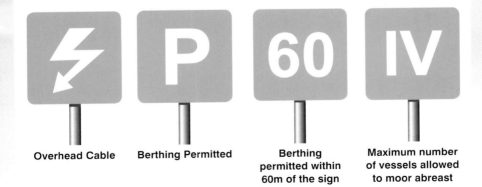

| Overhead Cable | Berthing Permitted | Berthing permitted within 60m of the sign | Maximum number of vessels allowed to moor abreast |

BUOYS AND FIXED MARKS

CHANNEL MARKERS

Channel markers come in various styles
but follow a theme; Red or Red and White,
square or inverted cones on the side of
the channel adjacent to the Right Bank.

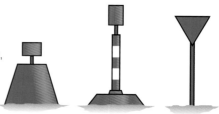

Green or Green and White cone
shapes on the side of the channel
adjacent to the Left Bank.

Green and Red 'hooped' marks are
'Bifurcation Marks' used where channels split
and re-join around obstructions in mid-stream.

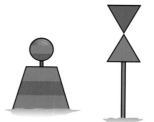

Yellow buoys denote 'restricted' areas. If the yellow buoy has a
red pennant on top then it denotes an area where navigation is prohibited.

OTHER BUOYS

On lakes and other broad waters you may encounter marks more usually found at sea.

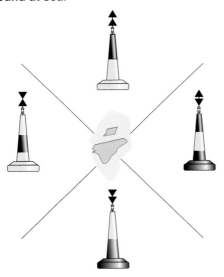

Yellow and Black 'Cardinal Marks' may be placed to the north, south, east or west of an obstruction as shown. You must navigate to the north of a North Cardinal, south of a South Cardinal, east of an East Cardinal and west of a West Cardinal to stay in safe water.

Black and Red 'Isolated Danger Marks' may be placed or moored on a 'small' obstruction, enabling you to navigate around it in safe water.

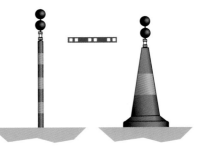

A White and Red 'Safe Water Mark' is most likely to mark the centre line of a navigable area.

LAND MARKS

The deep channel's route may be indicated by signs on the river, or canal, bank. Red and White square signs suggest that the channel is close to the Right Bank, while Green and White diamond shaped signs suggest that it runs nearer to the left.

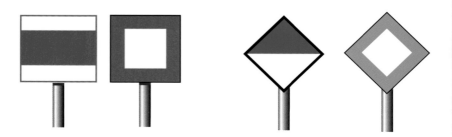

Places where the channel crosses from one side of the river to the other are marked on the bank by Yellow and Black boards or yellow crosses.

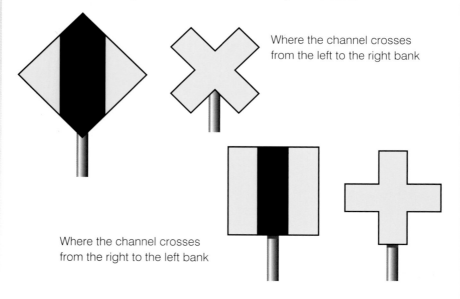

Where the channel crosses from the left to the right bank

Where the channel crosses from the right to the left bank

RULES OF THE ROAD

PRIORITIES

There are two types of vessel on the European inland waterways, SMALL CRAFT and NORMAL VESSELS.

■ 'Small craft' are all vessels under 20 metres long, except for Tugs, Ferries and Vessels licensed to carry more than 12 passengers. Most leisure boats will be 'small craft'.

■ 'Normal vessels' are all other craft. Most commercial vessels will be 'normal vessels'.

ALL SMALL CRAFT (even those sailing) MUST KEEP CLEAR OF NORMAL VESSELS.

The rules state that small craft 'shall stay out of Channels and prescribed traffic lanes whenever possible'. When that is impossible they shall navigate within 10 metres of the edge of the channel on their right hand side.

■ Motorised small craft give way to non-motorised and sailing small craft.

■ Non-motorised small craft give way to small craft sailing.

A vessel not required to 'give way' is usually the 'stand on' vessel and is expected to keep a steady course. In the confined inland waters, however, even the stand on vessel must be prepared to manoeuvre to avoid a collision.

VESSELS MEETING (from opposite directions)

Small craft meeting should each turn to Starboard and pass 'Port to Port'.

In most circumstances normal vessels will do the same, however, in rivers, normal vessels moving downstream (with the current) have priority over those going upstream. If a 'port to port' pass is not appropriate then the

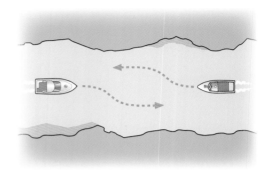

Upstream (give way) vessel can nominate a 'starboard to starboard' pass. In those circumstances the upstream vessel will show a Blue Board, or Scintillating White Light, on its starboard side. The Downstream vessel should repeat the signal as an acknowledgement.

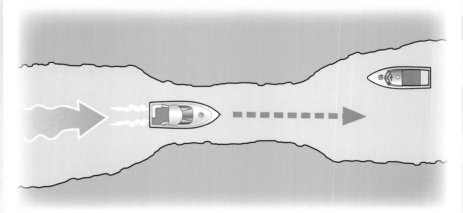

When vessels meet at a narrow channel then the downstream vessel has priority. An upstream vessel should allow any downstream vessels to clear the 'narrows' before entering. If an upstream vessel is already in the narrows an arriving downstream vessel must wait for the upstream vessel to pass through.

If small craft under sail meet then the one on starboard tack is the stand on vessel.

VESSELS CROSSING

If sailing vessels cross paths then if they are on opposite tacks, the port tack boat will give way. If they are on the same tacks then the windward boat will give way.

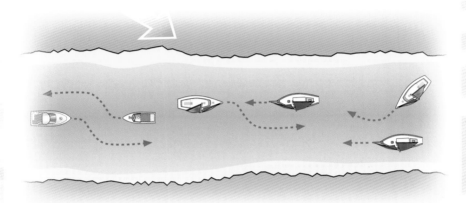

When motorised vessels cross paths then the vessel with the other on their starboard side should give way, unless that vessel is hard onto the starboard edge of the channel.

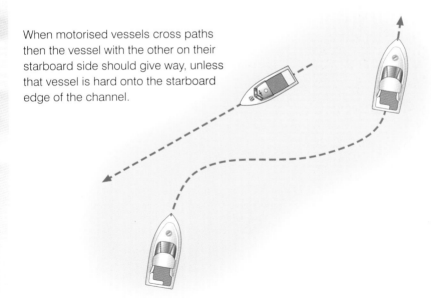

VESSELS OVERTAKING

■ Overtaking is only permitted when it can be carried out safely. An overtaken vessel should be prepared to slow down to speed up the manoeuvre.

■ An overtaking pass should be made on the port side of the overtaken vessel, though it is allowed on the starboard side when the waterway is particularly wide.

■ If the overtaken vessel needs to facilitate the manoeuvre then the overtaking vessel must seek permission using two long blasts on his horn followed by one short blast if he wants to overtake to starboard, or two short blasts if he wants to overtake to port. The overtaken vessel will give permission with one short blast if he wants the pass on his port side or two short blasts if he wants the pass to starboard. If he doesn't want the overtaking manoeuvre to happen he will give five short blasts on his horn.

VESSELS TURNING, LEAVING OR ENTERING A BERTH

■ Vessels should only turn, leave or enter berths and anchorages without causing other vessels to alter course or speed.

■ If however a normal vessel needs the co-operation of others to carry out such a manoeuvre, it will give a single long blast on its horn as a warning, followed by one short blast if it intends turning to starboard or two short blasts if it intends turning to port.

■ A normal vessel that requires others to alter course when leaving a berth will sound one short blast as a warning if vessels are approaching its starboard side or two short blasts if vessels are approaching its port side.

VESSELS LEAVING OR ENTERING A SIDE ARM OR HARBOUR

■ Flashing yellow lights at a Side Arm (branch canal or entry to a harbour), warn of normal vessels emerging. Vessels in the main stream must be prepared to manoeuvre to allow the movement.

■ Normal vessels entering or leaving a side arm will give three long blasts on their horns as a warning plus one short blast if they intend to turn to starboard or two short blasts if they intend turning to port.

■ If normal vessels intending to enter a side arm approach from opposite directions then the vessel pointing upstream has the right to enter first. You can expect a downstream vessel to make a full turn 'into the stream' before turning into the side arm pointing upstream.

■ Passage through junctions may be controlled by red and green traffic lights. Be prepared to manoeuvre to avoid vessels working under control of the lights.

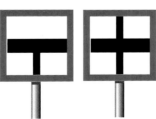

■ If the signs shown here are encountered then you may only emerge into the main stream when your manoeuvre will not cause another vessel to change course.

NAVIGATION LIGHTS

All vessels underway on the waterways after dark must carry 'Running' lights comprising a white stern light, green starboard light and red port light. Motorised vessels must also carry a white steaming light.

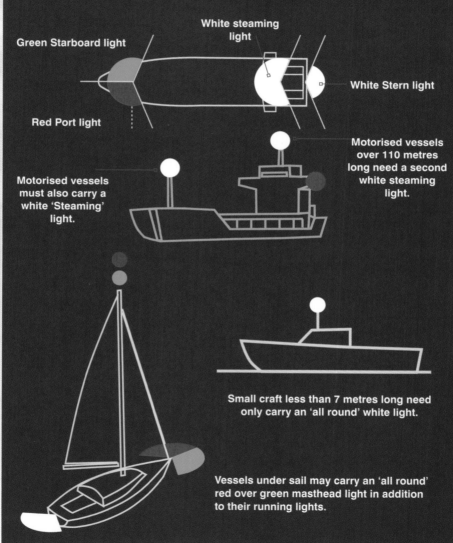

White steaming light

Green Starboard light

White Stern light

Red Port light

Motorised vessels must also carry a white 'Steaming' light.

Motorised vessels over 110 metres long need a second white steaming light.

Small craft less than 7 metres long need only carry an 'all round' white light.

Vessels under sail may carry an 'all round' red over green masthead light in addition to their running lights.

SPECIAL LIGHTS AND SHAPES

As well as the navigation lights there are many 'special' light combinations and day shapes, that tell you what a vessel is doing, or what its intentions are, and often, how best to avoid it.

Here are some of the most common and important.

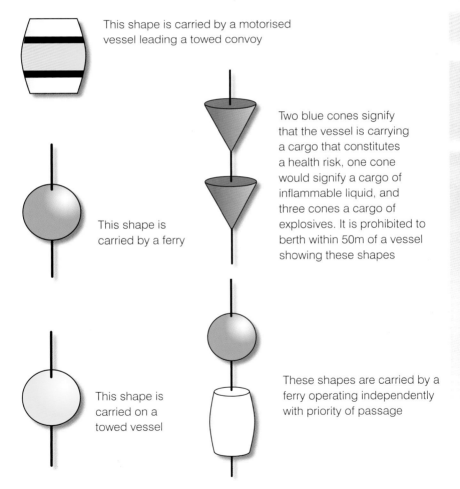

This shape is carried by a motorised vessel leading a towed convoy

This shape is carried by a ferry

Two blue cones signify that the vessel is carrying a cargo that constitutes a health risk, one cone would signify a cargo of inflammable liquid, and three cones a cargo of explosives. It is prohibited to berth within 50m of a vessel showing these shapes

This shape is carried on a towed vessel

These shapes are carried by a ferry operating independently with priority of passage

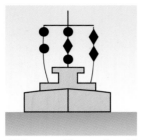 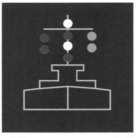 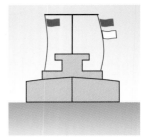

This vessel is restricted in its ability to manoeuvre (ball diamond ball). The safe side to pass is marked on its port side by two diamonds. The 'unsafe' side is marked by two balls. If you are approaching, leave it to Port.

This vessel is Protected against Wash, the clear passage is indicated by the red over white flags.

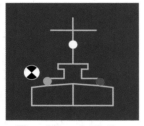 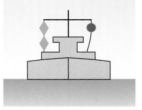 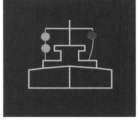

The white scintillating light on this 'upstream vessel' shows that it is holding to the right bank. Pass starboard to starboard.

The red ball on this vessel indicates that it is At Work. The two green diamonds show the safe side to pass, so if you are approaching, leave it to starboard.

A yellow bi-cone is shown on a passenger vessel under 20m carrying more than 12 passengers.

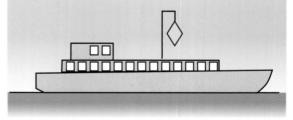

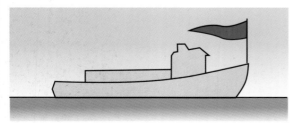

A red pennant is carried by a vessel enjoying priority of passage.

<u>ERRATA</u>

Page 22: The middle picture of the top row should have a green starboard navigation light and a red port navigation light.

Page 23: The right-hand picture of the middle row should have a white steaming light above the top red light.

Page 23: The text below the left-hand picture of the bottom row should read: *These lights signify a ferry moving independently, frontal aspect.*

Page 23: The right-hand picture of the bottom row should have a green starboard navigation light and a red port navigation light.

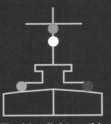

The blue light on this motorised vessel approaching head on, indicates that it is carrying inflammable liquids. (Two blue lights would signify a cargo hazardous to health, and three would signify explosives).

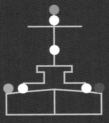

The triangular arrangement of steaming lights plus running lights indicates that this is a pusher unit approaching head on, the blue light shows that it is carrying inflammable liquid.

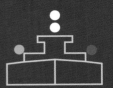

Two steaming lights plus running lights indicate a motorised vessel leading a towed convoy.

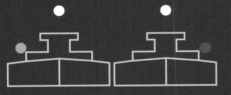

The horizontal arrangement of two steaming lights plus running lights suggests two vessels travelling abreast, approaching head on.

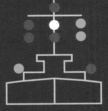

The red white red lights show a vessel restricted in its ability to manoeuvre. The two red lights show the unsafe side, while the two green lights indicate the safe side to pass.

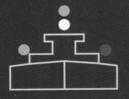

These lights signify a ferry moving independently, starboard aspect.

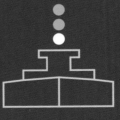

These lights signify a ferry moving independently with priority of passage.

CONDUCT AT LOCKS

■ Slow down and don't overtake on the approach to a lock. The boat master should contact the lock operator on the appropriate VHF channel and follow instructions. Stop short of any red/white boards or red lights. Entry to the lock is on a first come first served basis, but normal vessels have priority over small craft. So small craft can expect to be called in behind normal vessels.

■ In the lock, make fast within the marked zones without bumping the lock or any of its gear. Once secured, turn off your engine until you are ready to leave.

■ While in the lock your anchor must remain fully raised, and any removable fenders (use of fenders is mandatory) must be buoyant.

Signals used at locks are straightforward:
Red and White boards or red lights for STOP
Red and Green lights together for GET READY
Green and White boards or green lights for GO

CONDUCT AT BRIDGES

MOVEABLE BRIDGES

Look for a sign giving a VHF channel and take note of instructions from Bridge Staff. If there are signal boards or lights then they will be mostly the same as for locks:

Red and White boards or red lights for STOP
Red and Green lights together for GET READY
Green and White boards or green lights for GO

 A single or two red lights vertically arranged, indicates the suspension of navigation, for short or long periods. However a yellow light in association with the the reds allows passage for vessels with sufficient air-draught. One yellow light allows passage from both directions, while two allow one-way traffic only.

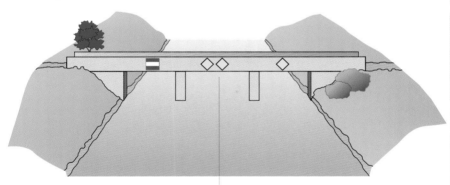

FIXED BRIDGES

If the navigable width under a span is 'narrow' then downstream vessels have priority of passage as in narrow channels. Yellow Diamonds or yellow lights indicate the recommended passages, where one diamond/light stands for two-way traffic, and two diamonds/lights indicate one-way traffic only.

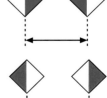

Pairs of green and white diamonds recommend safe passage between the signs, while red and white diamonds indicate that there is No Passage outside of the signs.

BERTHING

Berthing is not allowed in places where the berthed vessel will cause an obstruction to approaching traffic. Here are 9 examples of places where vessels should not berth.

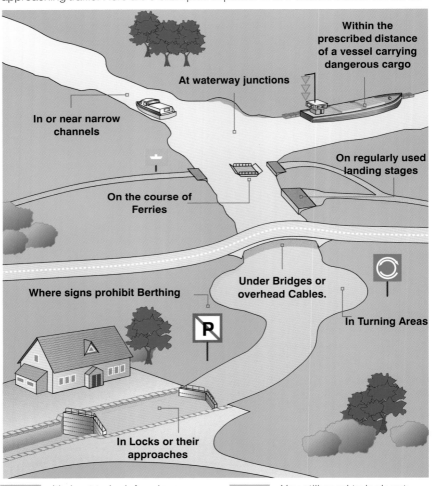

Within the prescribed distance of a vessel carrying dangerous cargo

At waterway junctions

In or near narrow channels

On regularly used landing stages

On the course of Ferries

Where signs prohibit Berthing

Under Bridges or overhead Cables.

In Turning Areas

In Locks or their approaches

It's best to look for places where berthing is positively allowed, for instance where you see one of these signs.

You still need to look out for restrictions, such as a limit to the number of boats allowed to 'raft up'.

SOUND SIGNALS

The CEVNI rules include a series of sound signals that are quite different from those used at sea. Here is a list of the main ones. Because 'small vessels' must give way to all 'normal vessels', not all of the signals are appropriate for small craft to use. Those that small craft can use are noted in red.

■	I am steering to (or holding to) starboard
■ ■	I am steering to (or holding to) port
■ ■ ■	I am going astern
■ ■ ■ ■	I am unable to manoeuvre
■ ■ ■ ■ ■	Do not overtake me
∎ ∎ ∎ ∎ ∎ ∎	Imminent danger of collision (six or more very short blasts)

▬	Caution
▬ ■	I am turning (or turning about) to starboard
▬ ■ ■	I am turning (or turning about) to port
▬ ▬ ■	I wish to overtake on your starboard side
▬ ▬ ■ ■	I wish to overtake on your port side
▬ ▬ ▬	I am exiting from a port or side arm and crossing the waterway
▬ ▬ ▬ ■	I am exiting/entering a port or side arm and turning to starboard
▬ ▬ ▬ ■ ■	I am exiting/entering a port or side arm and turning to port

DISTRESS SIGNALS

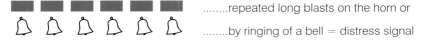

........repeated long blasts on the horn or

........by ringing of a bell = distress signal

DISTRESS SIGNALS

The following nine signals are used to indicate that a vessel is in DISTRESS and requires IMMEDIATE ASSISTANCE!

1. Six or more short blasts on the horn
2. A flag or other suitable object waved in a circle.
3. A light waved in a circle.
4. A square flag having below or above it a ball or circular shape.
5. Red rocket flares or star shells
6. Hand held red flare
7. Flames on deck
8. A light flashing SOS in Morse Code
9. Slow up and down movement of both arms

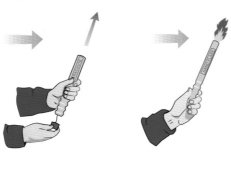

GLOSSARY

air-draught	vertical clearance height between vessel and bridge
authorisations	signs, flags or lights authorising passage
bifurcation marks	marks and buoys used where channels split and re-join around obstructions in mid-channel
Cardinal marks	marks and buoys placed to north, south, east and west of obstruction
distress signal	indicates vessel is in imminent danger and requires immediate assistance
'give way' vessel	vessel required to allow free passage to another
ICC	International Certificate of Competence – qualification required when sailing as master of vessel abroad
indications	signs providing information and indicating permitted activities
isolated danger marks	marks and buoys indicating location of 'small' obstructions
land marks	signs on bank of waterway indicating deep channel route
lateral buoys	buoys marking river channel
locks	installations to raise or lower vessels to a higher or lower level of waterway
mandatory signs	signs that must be obeyed
navigation lights	lights required to be shown by vessels at night
'normal vessels'	all craft other than 'small craft' (see small craft)
prohibitions	signs describing action you must not take
pusher unit	barge pushed along by vessel at stern
rafting up	where two or more vessels berth alongside each other
recommendations	signs signalling the best way to proceed
restrictions	signs detailing physical restrictions, or limitations to navigation
running lights	lights required to be shown by vessels underway at night
safe water marks	mark centre line of navigable area
scintillating white light	flashing navigation light on vessel
side arm	branch canal or entry to a harbour
'small craft'	vessels under 20 metres long, except for tugs, ferries and vessels licensed to carry more than 12 passengers
'stand on' vessel	vessel having priority of passage over another
steaming light	light required to be shown by motorised vessels underway at night
tacking	sailing in windward direction on zig-zag course

SAMPLE TEST PAPER

In the UK candidates for an 'Inland' International Certificate of Competence will be asked to complete a test on the CEVNI rules. The test will comprise 14 questions, with multiple-choice answers. Here is a sample test paper.

RYA

CEVNI TEST for ICC (INLAND)

Select one answer for each question. Write a, b, c, or d as appropriate against the relevant question number on the answer sheet.
DO NOT MARK THIS PAPER.

1

1000
10

This sign means:

a. Headroom limit 10m in 1000m
b. Width of channel 10m in 1000m
c. Speed limit 10kph in 1000m
d. Channel 10m from the bank in 1000m

2

This sign means:

a. Bridge works ahead
b. No passage through bridge
c. Do not make wash
d. Slow, bends ahead

3

This sign means:

a. One way traffic
b. Keep to starboard side of channel
c. Priority to upstream traffic
d. No overtaking or passing

4

These lights signify:

a. Don't make any wash
b. Sound your horn
c. Passage for pleasure craft only
d. Prolonged stoppage

5

This sign means:

a. Sharp bends ahead
b. Channel moves to starboard
c. Cross channel to starboard
d. Keep to starboard side of channel

6

These lights signify:

a. Beware - vessels leaving side arm to port
b. Make no waves
c. Passage for vessels of reduced height – one-way traffic
d. Passage for pleasure craft only

7

Buoyage:

a. Marks an obstacle on the right side of the navigation
b. Marks an obstacle on the left side of the navigation
c. Bifurcation of the channel – pass to either side
d. Restricted water depth

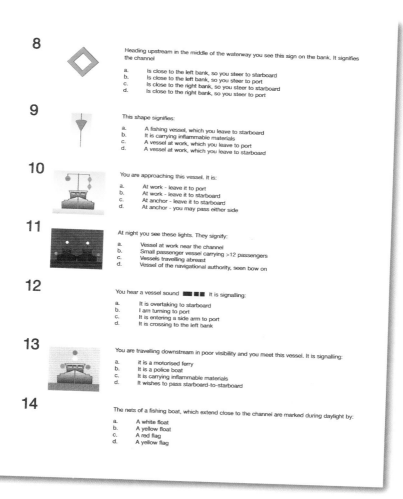

8

Heading upstream in the middle of the waterway you see this sign on the bank. It signifies the channel

a. Is close to the left bank, so you steer to starboard
b. Is close to the left bank, so you steer to port
c. Is close to the right bank, so you steer to starboard
d. Is close to the right bank, so you steer to port

9

This shape signifies:

a. A fishing vessel, which you leave to starboard
b. It is carrying inflammable materials
c. A vessel at work, which you leave to port
d. A vessel at work, which you leave to starboard

10

You are approaching this vessel. It is:

a. At work - leave it to port
b. At work - leave it to starboard
c. At anchor - leave it to starboard
d. At anchor - you may pass either side

11

At night you see these lights. They signify:

a. Vessel at work near the channel
b. Small passenger vessel carrying >12 passengers
c. Vessels travelling abreast
d. Vessel of the navigational authority, seen bow on

12

You hear a vessel sound ▄▄ ▄▄ ▄▄ It is signalling:

a. It is overtaking to starboard
b. I am turning to port
c. It is entering a side arm to port
d. It is crossing to the left bank

13

You are travelling downstream in poor visibility and you meet this vessel. It is signalling:

a. it is a motorised ferry
b. It is a police boat
c. It is carrying inflammable materials
d. It wishes to pass starboard-to-starboard

14

The nets of a fishing boat, which extend close to the channel are marked during daylight by:

a. A white float
b. A yellow float
c. A red flag
d. A yellow flag

The answers to the sample paper are:
1C; 2C; 3B; 4D; 5B; 6C; 7C; 8B; 9B; 10A; 11C; 12B; 13C; 14B

INDEX

IT'S ALL ABOUT YOU AND THE BOATING YOU DO

RYA MEMBERSHIP APPLICATION

Be part of it

One of boating's biggest attractions is its freedom from rules and regulations. As an RYA member you'll play an active part in keeping it that way, as well as benefiting from free expert advice and information, plus discounts on a wide range of boating products, charts and publications.

To join the RYA, please complete the application form below and send it to The Membership Department, RYA, RYA House, Ensign Way, Hamble, Southampton, Hampshire SO31 4YA. You can also join online at www.rya.org.uk, or by phoning the membership department on +44 (0) 23 8060 4159. Whichever way you choose to apply, you can save money by paying by Direct Debit. A Direct Debit instruction is on the back of this form.

	Title	Forename	Surname	Gender	Date of Birth
Applicant ❶					/ /
Applicant ❷					/ /
Applicant ❸					/ /
Applicant ❹					/ /

Address

Post Code

E-mail Applicant ❶	
E-mail Applicant ❷	
E-mail Applicant ❸	
E-mail Applicant ❹	

Home Tel

Day Time Tel

Mobile Tel

Type of membership required (Tick Box)

Junior (0-11)	Annual rate £5 or **£5 if paying by Direct Debit**	
Youth (12-17)	Annual rate £14 or **£11 if paying by Direct Debit**	
Under 25	Annual rate £25 or **£22 if paying by Direct Debit**	
Personal	Annual rate £43 or **£39 if paying by Direct Debit**	
Family*	Annual rate £63 or **£59 if paying by Direct Debit**	

Save money by completing the Direct Debit form overleaf

Please number up to three boating interests in order, with number one being your principal interest

Yacht Racing	Yacht Cruising	Dinghy Cruising
Personal Watercraft	Sportboats & RIBs	Windsurfing
Powerboat Racing	Canal Cruising	River Cruising

Dinghy Racing

* Family Membership: 2 adults plus any under 18s all living at the same address. Prices valid until 30/9/2011 One discount voucher is accepted for individual memberships, and two discount vouchers are accepted for family membership.

IMPORTANT In order to provide you with membership benefits the details provided by you on this form and in the course of your membership will be maintained on a database.
If you do not wish to receive information on member services and benefits please tick here ☐ By applying for membership of the RYA you agree to be bound by the RYA's standard terms and conditions (copies on request or at www.rya.org.uk)

Signature _____ Date ___ / ___ / ___

Source Code

Joining Point Code

RYA
Be part of it

PAY BY DIRECT DEBIT – AND SAVE MONEY

GET MORE FROM
YOUR
BOATING
SUPPORT THE
RYA

Instructions to your Bank or Building Society to pay by Direct Debit

Please fill in the form and send to:

Membership Department, Royal Yachting Association, RYA House, Ensign Way, Hamble, Southampton, Hampshire SO31 4YA.

Name and full postal address of your Bank/Building Society

To the Manager   Bank/Building Society

Address

Postcode

Name(s) of Account Holder(s)

Branch Sort Code

[ ] [ ] - [ ] [ ] - [ ] [ ]

Bank/Building Society Account Number

[ ] [ ] [ ] [ ] [ ] [ ] [ ] [ ]

Originator's Identification Number

| 9 | 5 | 5 | 2 | 1 | 3 |

RYA Membership Number (For office use only)

 DIRECT Debit

Instructions to your Bank or Building Society

Please pay Royal Yachting Association Direct Debits from the account detailed in this instruction subject to the safeguards assured by The Direct Debit Guarantee. I understand that this instruction may remain with the Royal Yachting Association and, if so, details will be passed electronically to my Bank/Building Society.

Signature(s)

Date: [D] [D] / [M] [M] / [Y] [Y] [Y] [Y]